Classic Tales Completely Ruined by Cabbage

Book One:

Goldilocks and the Three Bears

written by ANDY DOMEK illustrated by MARCUS CUTLER

To Emma, Sophie, Edie, and Ben—

Laughter is lovely and I love your laughs. And you.

-A.D.

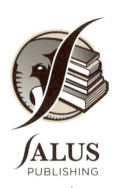

Copyright © 2020 by Andy Domek
Illustrations Copyright © 2020 by Marcus Cutler
All rights reserved. This is a work of fiction. The events and characters described here are products of the author's imagination. No part of this book may be used or reproduced in any manner whatsoever without written permission by the publisher, except in the case of brief quotations embodied in critical articles or reviews. For more information, contact Salus Publishing LLC, 5406 Crossings Dr. Ste 102-353, Rocklin, CA 95677.

First edition December 2020.

ISBN (Paperback): 978-1-7335426-1-6

Published by:
Salus Publishing LLC
5406 Crossings Dr.
Ste 102-353
Rocklin, CA 95677

Printed in Canada by Hemlock Printers.
This book is printed on 100% PCW FSC® Recycled paper.
We stand with the trees.
www.SalusPublishing.com
Iacta alea est.

Andy Domek is a writer who loves bad jokes and dad jokes, and often repeats himself. He loves to grow tomatoes up makeshift garden contraptions, experiment in his kitchen and harbors an intense dislike of mashed turnips. Andy lives in West Sacramento, California with his family.

Marcus Cutler hates cabbage but once had to eat an entire plate of it out of politeness. When not being forced into awful meals, he likes to draw, play with his daughters, and high-five his wife. Marcus lives in Ontario, Canada.

Stay tuned for the next perfectly good fairytale completely ruined by cabbage.

Once upon a time a family of bears lived in a cozy little house at the edge of a vast forest.

Papa Bear was up early one summer morning. So he made his family's favorite breakfast—porridge with juicy blackberries. And on the side, fresh cabbage from their garden.

He filled three bowls with steaming porridge: one big, one medium and one little. Then he set each bowl on the table. Baby Bear added the juicy berries on top. Mama Bear set out the crisp cabbage. The porridge was too hot to eat right away, so the trio went for a walk while it cooled.

As the Bear family sauntered through a nearby meadow filled with flowers, a girl from a glade over the hill strolled by. Her name was Goldilocks and her tummy was not happy. She had skipped breakfast so she could scamper outside.

Goldilocks stopped in front of the Bear family's home. She did not know who lived there, but the tantalizing aroma of blackberries and porridge tickled her nose and it led her right up to their front door.

"Maybe whoever lives here will share some of whatever smells soooooo good," Goldilocks thought, as she rapped on the heavy wooden door.

But the only response was a grumbly growl from her tummy.
"Hmmmmm," she smiled. "HELLO!!!!" No reply.

Goldilocks pushed open the door and followed her nose to the Bears' breakfast. She grabbed an enormous spoon and shoveled a GIANT bite of porridge into her mouth from the biggest bowl.

"OOWWWWWWWIIIIEEEEE," she howled.

Next, she tried Mama's medium-sized bowl and Baby Bear's small bowl. All of it was WAY too hot, since the Bears had only just walked out the door.

Hungry and with a sore tongue, Goldilocks noticed the cabbage. Now, nothing green made it onto Goldilocks' Top 50 List of Favorite Foods. But, her tummy was willing to make an exception. So she nibbled a small, cabbage-y bite from Baby Bear's plate. Not terrible.

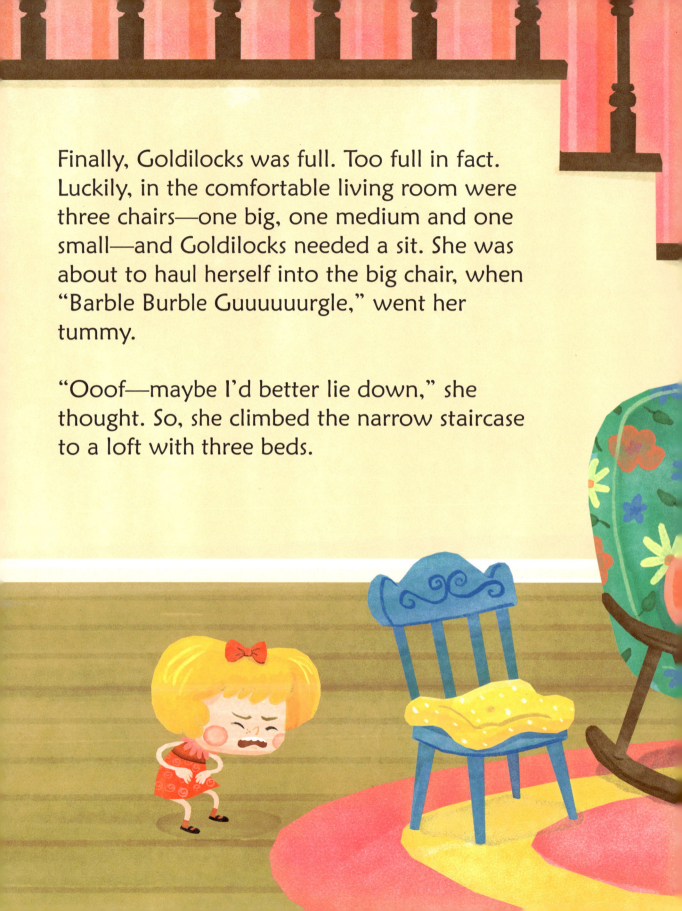

Finally, Goldilocks was full. Too full in fact. Luckily, in the comfortable living room were three chairs—one big, one medium and one small—and Goldilocks needed a sit. She was about to haul herself into the big chair, when "Barble Burble Guuuuuurgle," went her tummy.

"Ooof—maybe I'd better lie down," she thought. So, she climbed the narrow staircase to a loft with three beds.

The huge bed was rock hard! She and her tummy could not get comfy. The medium bed was as squishy as a jellyfish-but Goldilocks' gut did not approve. Finally, she crawled into the smallest bed, which was just right. There she lay clutching her ballooning and burbling belly.

Goldilocks meant to get up and leave, but just felt too awful. Nevertheless, when she heard loud and heavy footsteps tromp back into the kitchen…

"Change of plans!" Goldilocks thought as she dove under the biggest bed.

"GURGLE GURGLE!" went her tummy.

The Bears were now so hungry that Papa and Mama Bear didn't notice the bites missing from their porridge. Baby Bear noticed that the cabbage was gone.

But the plump blackberries were so sweet, he soon forgot about it. When their bowls were empty and Bear bellies full, the family meandered over to their chairs and began to read.

Goldilocks snuck to the top of the stairs and peeked down. One glimpse of Papa Bear's GINORMOUS teeth (he was only yawning) made her whole body tremble. Which did not help her tummy. In fact, those shakes let loose a teensy, tiny…

"Pbbbsssssrrrrt!!!" said Goldilocks' butt.
"Oh no!" she gasped, "At least it was quiet…" But then,

"What was that???"
whispered Mama Bear.

"It came from upstairs,"
said Baby Bear.

"It sounded like someone tooted their horn. A real bum shaker. Pantaloon trumpet if you will," chuckled Papa Bear. "But, if it truly was indeed a gaseous tootilation of that size, surely we'd have smelled it by…"

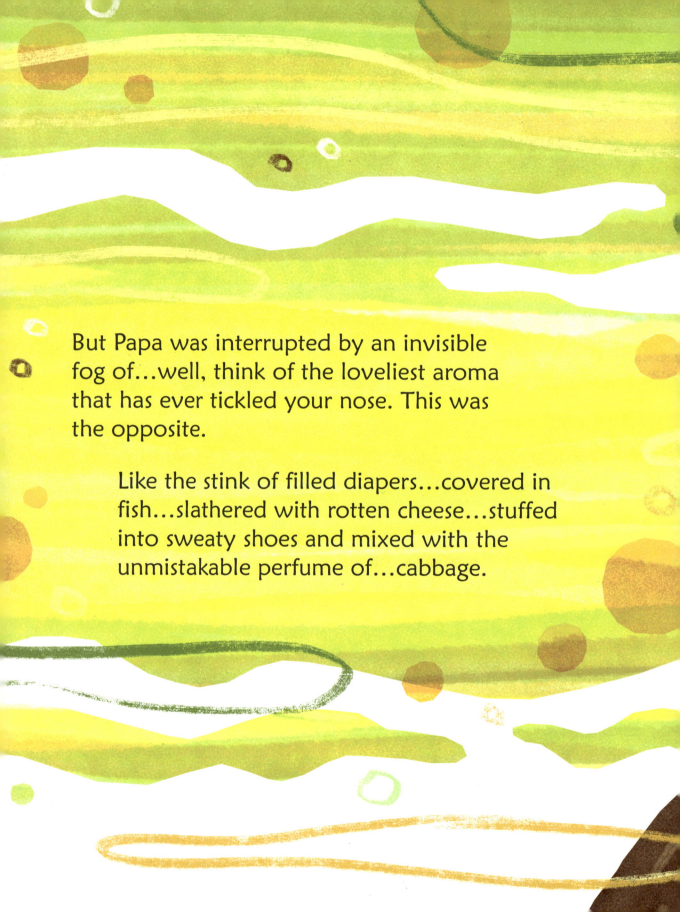

But Papa was interrupted by an invisible fog of…well, think of the loveliest aroma that has ever tickled your nose. This was the opposite.

Like the stink of filled diapers…covered in fish…slathered with rotten cheese…stuffed into sweaty shoes and mixed with the unmistakable perfume of…cabbage.

Baby Bear retched.
Mama Bear gagged.
"That's it!" said Papa Bear
(who was retching and gagging).
"Someone's in our house!"

"Ok, time to panic!" Goldilocks yelped. She threw herself down the stairs two by two—each fart like a duck's quack on every footfall.

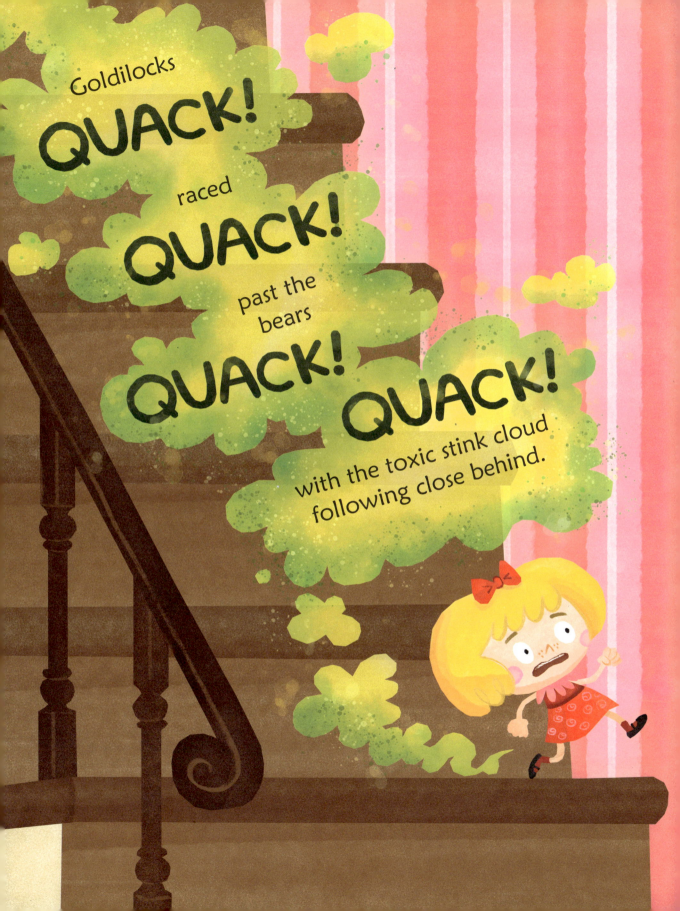

"Should we go after her?" asked Baby Bear. "No! We might catch her, and we've had enough stink to last all month!" Mama Bear replied.

The bear family went back to their reading. With the windows WIDE open, of course.